T0339508

Sustainability, Conservation, and Creativity

By examining how small communities have dealt with forces of change and have sought to maintain themselves over time, this book offers pointers and lessons for conservation practices at all levels of society.

"Sustainability" has become an increasingly popular term as a signal of concerns with long-term environmental consequences of human actions. Sustainability as a goal has started to replace "development" as a way of describing policies that go beyond the concept of increasing commercial production or making monetary profits from enterprises. By focusing on topical case histories on agricultural activity, stock-keeping, cash cropping, mining, and renewable energy, the authors highlight how ethnographic studies can and should inform policy decisions at both local and global levels.

This book will be of great interest to students and scholars of applied anthropology, sociology, and development studies.

Pamela J. Stewart (Strathern) is Co-Director of the Cromie Burn Research Unit and Senior Research Associate at the University of Pittsburgh, USA, and Honorary Associate Professor at the Australian National University.

Andrew J. Strathern is the Andrew W. Mellon Professor of Anthropology at the University of Pittsburgh, USA, and Honorary Professor at the Australian National University.

Routledge Focus on Environment and Sustainability

Productivity and Innovation in SMEs
Creating Competitive Advantage in Singapore and Southeast Asia
Azad Bali, Peter McKiernan, Christopher Vas and Peter Waring

Climate Adaptation Finance and Investment in California
Jesse M. Keenan

Negotiating the Environment
Civil Society, Globalisation and the UN
Lauren E. Eastwood

Carbon Inequality
The Role of the Richest in Climate Change
Dario Kenner

The UNESCO Manual for Developing Intercultural Competencies
Story Circles
Darla K. Deardorff

Design for Sustainability
A Multi-level Framework from Products to Socio-technical Systems
Fabrizio Ceschin and İdil Gaziulusoy

Sustainability, Conservation, and Creativity
Ethnographic Learning from Small-scale Practices
Pamela J. Stewart and Andrew J. Strathern

For more information about this series, please visit: https://www.routledge.com/Routledge-Focus-on-Environment-and-Sustainability/book-series/RFES

Sustainability, Conservation, and Creativity

Ethnographic Learning from
Small-scale Practices

**Pamela J. Stewart and
Andrew J. Strathern**

Routledge
Taylor & Francis Group

LONDON AND NEW YORK

First published 2020
by Routledge
2 Park Square, Milton Park, Abingdon, Oxon OX14 4RN

and by Routledge
605 Third Avenue, New York, NY 10017

First issued in paperback 2021

Routledge is an imprint of the Taylor & Francis Group, an informa business

Publisher's Note
The publisher has gone to great lengths to ensure the quality of this reprint
but points out that some imperfections in the original copies may be
apparent.

British Library Cataloguing-in-Publication Data
A catalogue record for this book is available from the British Library

Library of Congress Cataloging-in-Publication Data
A catalog record has been requested for this book

ISBN 13: 978-1-03-224028-2 (pbk)
ISBN 13: 978-1-138-31543-3 (hbk)

DOI: 10.4324/9780429456312

Typeset in Times New Roman
by Deanta Global Publishing Services, Chennai, India

To Rowan and Birch for sustainable living

Contents

About the authors

Pamela J. Stewart (Strathern) and **Andrew J. Strathern** are a wife-and-husband research team who are based in the Department of Anthropology, University of Pittsburgh, and co-direct the Cromie Burn Research Unit. They are frequently invited international lecturers and have worked with numbers of museums to assist these organizations in documenting their collections from the Pacific. They have worked and lived in many parts of the world. Stewart and Strathern have published over 50 books, over 80 prefaces for other authors' scholarly books, and hundreds of articles, book chapters, and essays on their research in the Pacific (mainly Papua New Guinea and the South-West Pacific region, e.g., Samoa, Cook Islands, and Fiji); Asia (mainly Taiwan, and also including Mainland China, Inner Mongolia, and Japan); and Europe (primarily Scotland, Ireland, Germany, and the European Union countries in general); and also Norway, New Zealand, and Australia. Stewart and Strathern's current research includes the new subfield of Disaster Anthropology that they have been developing for many years. They are the series editors for the new *Palgrave Studies in Disaster Anthropology*. Also, the topics of Cosmological Landscapes; Ritual Studies; Political Peace-Making; Comparative Anthropological Studies of Disasters and Climatic Change; Language, Culture and Cognitive Science; and Scottish and Irish Studies are ones that they continue to investigate. They are on the editorial boards of the journals *Shaman* and *Religion and Society* and they co-edit the *Journal of Ritual Studies*. They are the co-leaders of the University of Pittsburgh, Study Abroad program *Pitt in the Pacific*, which they developed from their contacts in the Pacific, especially at the University of Otago in Dunedin, New Zealand.

Their webpages, listing publications, and other scholarly activities are http://www.pitt.edu/~strather/ and http://www.StewartStrathern.pitt.edu/.

Acknowledgments

We would like to thank the reviewers of our manuscript who provided their time and expertise. We also wish to thank the staff at the Press who have been attentive and assisted us in the production of this book. We also wish to thank the many people that we have worked with in our global traverses, stays, and movements. Also, many people have worked with us in the field and at institutions that we have worked at while conducting research and lecturing. Further information on our research, writings, and collaborations can be found on the internet and at a few of our own webpages:

http://www.stewartstrathern.pitt.edu/
http://www.pitt.edu/~strather/
http://www.pitt.edu/~strather/sandspublicat.htm

Our *Journal of Ritual Studies* (Stewart and Strathern, Editors in Chief, web and Facebook Page):

https://www.pitt.edu/~strather/journal.htm
https://www.facebook.com/ritualstudies

1 Conceptual orientations

This book is an exploration of a topic that is of great importance in the world today: how can the use of resources by humans continue in a sustainable way when the overall emphasis appears to be on increased production and consumption and potentially therefore on the unsustainable depletion of resources? Answers to this question inevitably depend on the attitudes and values of the human actors involved. "Sustainability" as a concept can be framed differently by different people, even by individuals within a given cultural milieu. As a concept it is therefore both malleable and moot. The issues surrounding it include the following. When we say that a practice is sustainable, do we mean that it continues unchanged? If it changes, has it been sustained? What ranges of time do we need to take into account here? Since one practice may advantage some actors and disadvantage others, for whom are we reckoning sustainability? Ecology also involves the study of interaction between actors in a wider web of relationships, so what is sustainable for humans may be unsustainable for other species. Finally, does "sustainable" equate with "optimal"? In contemporary discussions, it may be that the answer to this point is yes, since "sustainable development" is often held up as a desirable goal to achieve, but this is not an absolute matter. A practice may be sustainable, but at what cost? In short, the word sustainable turns out to be complex and even awkward to pin down and make it operational. In this book, therefore, we use it as a pointer to discussions centering on a cluster of issues about the viability of practices and the social values attached to them. We can accept in broader terms that all practices need to have built into them the capacity to persist over time and space, and we can speak of this capacity as "sustainability", always bearing in mind that an ecological approach demands that we realize that what keeps one entity going may entail the death of another. A truly balanced ecological approach would therefore be one that minimized such a zero-sum situation. However, species loss is such an established ecological situation that it is impossible to guarantee such balance, notwithstanding the fact that efforts to conserve a particular species of plants or animals can be profitably entered into and are important in their own right.

In seeking a model for studying issues of sustainability, therefore, we identify the following parts:

1. First, the definition of an ecosystem, specifying this domain of interactions.
2. Second, the recognition that one system may be enmeshed in a wider web of relations.
3. Third, that sustainability has to be thought of in terms of time and space so that its extent is both historical and geographical.
4. Fourth, that human agency is involved at all levels of scale, as well as environmental factors stemming from conditions of the planet as a whole, including climate change.
5. Fifth, that when a crisis of sustainability arises, ingenuity and creativity of response to such a crisis is crucial.
6. Sixth, that this creativity will indicate the powers of resilience and recovery from any crisis that is experienced.
7. Seventh, that the mode of recovery, or the lack of it, becomes the marker for sustainability.
8. Eighth, that we always bear in mind the degree to which recovery is encompassing or partial, both in relation to humans and in relation to other species in our biosphere.

With these modeling pointers, we will enter into case materials, relevant to the issues of sustainability outlined here. However, some further clarifications of our viewpoints are necessary.

We recognize that energy extraction is a basic requirement for all species. The human capacity for fuel extraction has been driven over time by technology, and notably by industrial development and its complex and elaborate machinery. This development builds on elementary human needs, such as for shelter, food, and mobility, and creates a massive superstructure that then requires sustainable maintenance in itself. In solving one problem, for example, the need to produce food, complex technology creates others, for example how to afford the machinery needed and how to handle issues of pollution, depletion, and overuse. Businesses are then built onto this situation, escalating both the solutions and the problems. Sustainability moves in this way from an elemental human need, for food say, into a complex set of social problems. In other words, sustainability cannot be considered only in material or biological terms but must involve a continuous cross-over between the material and the social dimensions of life.

We recognize also that increases in the scale of social units and contexts that have emerged as a result of industrial and post-industrial development make the analysis of sustainability more complex. Cities are the sites where problems and solutions to them obviously meet or fail to meet. Can we see a city or a set of cities as an *ecosystem*? Cities are located in space and have their official boundaries, but they are also inextricably joined with other sites in the world. For a city, the question of sustainability has to be phrased in starkly monetary terms. Where will the money come from to address social and material issues? The essence of an ecosystem approach is to see how factors are balanced or imbalanced and their effects. For cities, this question is very hard to compute, but in financial terms, it is also very much to the forefront in planning. In terms of sustainability, carbon-neutral solutions are obviously at a premium, but they are not always feasible. Cities have long-standing environmental problems, in terms of air pollution and contamination of the earth, and these need to be addressed in order to bring an *ecosystems* viewpoint back into plans for sustainability.

Generally, then, what can an ethnographic approach contribute to approaching these problems? An ethnographic approach is admirably, if not uniquely, suited to understanding the viewpoints of the social actors themselves, because it starts from observations of behavior and from conversational dialogue with the people. This method has been followed in time-honored traditions for small-scale societies, but it is equally applicable everywhere. Every large-scale context contains within it numerous small-scale levels. People operate at the smaller-scale levels, they think locally, even in global contexts. Large-scale problems begin to be solved by ingenious co-operative action at smaller scales. Cities encompass numerous interlinked localities, whose concerns have to be recognized and harnessed. In other words, a city may comprise a number of "villages" or village-like units. They are not monolithic. Local initiatives are important, such as in establishing urban gardens or local food markets. In our essay "What Is Sustainable?" (Strathern and Stewart 2017) we explore some of the questions and issues of sustainability.

Another issue is the degree of comparison that can be entered into. Given what we have just outlined, there is no reason to reject comparisons that cross over between scales of geographical regions of the world. Renewable energy schemes in Scotland, for example, exist at small-scale levels as well as more broadly. Cultural attitudes and values are always in play. We take two examples from parts of the world where we have conducted research for several decades: Papua New Guinea and Scotland (see, for example, Stewart and Strathern, 2002a, 2010). The effects of a new cash crop in parts of Papua New Guinea can from this viewpoint be compared with the effects of a wind turbine program in Scotland that also introduces wind turbines as a "new crop", enhancing the sustainability of one set of practices and perhaps reducing the sustainability of others. Scientists may not be accustomed to this mode of reasoning, but if we are to broaden our outlook, we need to become versed in cross-cultural analogies of this kind.

Finally, here, we repeat what we indicated in our opening sentence, that this book is an initial *exploration*, done from a certain perspective. Its aim is not encyclopedic. Its purpose is not to review all the literature on the topic. It is rather to bring to bear our field experiences and those of others on a topic of obvious importance today, and to offer some specific insights stemming from an ethnographic and anthropological approach, highlighting the creativity of people in coping with environmental or ecological problems. (See, for example, Feinberg, 2010, for an excellent study along these lines, based on his long-term fieldwork in the island of Anuta.)

2 Perceptions and practices in Papua New Guinea: the Duna case

One part of creativity relates to the basic cultural perceptions of reality that inform peoples' views of the world. Do people have an intrinsically conservationist attitude to their use of resources? When do they become aware that there is or may be an ecological problem with their access to resources? The Duna people of Hela Province in the Southern Highlands of Papua New Guinea, with whom we have worked for many years, provide some striking answers to such a question. We have carried out firsthand fieldwork among these people and published two books on them (Stewart and Strathern 2002a, Strathern and Stewart 2004). Male leaders of kin groups among the Duna keep elaborate knowledge of genealogies running for up to fourteen generations as a record of the group's identity, and its historical presence in the landscape. Each large group is thought to have originated from a powerful ancestor, part human part spirit, who is often also said to have migrated into the area from a distant place, such as Oksapmin, across the great Strickland River that marks the northern boundary of Duna settlements. These powerful founding characters can be seen as injecting strength into the land. After a full set of generations this initial strength is held to be waning and with it the fertility of the soil. Duna therefore perceived a horizon of potential unsustainability in their lifeworld, and they had developed an elaborate ritual complex to deal with their perceived situation. When they felt that fertility and life force was decreasing, they set in motion a series of ritualized actions to restore vitality. This ritual series was called *rindi kiniya*: setting the ground to rights, repairing the ground, restoring it. At intervals of time after the founding of a group, people expected to find sacred stones in their ground, indicating that an ancestor wanted to manifest himself and appeared in this shape to induce his descendants to set up a shrine where they could sacrifice pigs to honor him. People said that an ancestor might want to "come up" to the surface of the ground in this way five generations after his death and burial. In particular the stones that "came up" in this way were seen as the petrified hearts of the ancestors in question, thus incontrovertible manifestations of their identity and agency, calling on their descendants to recognize them and emplace them in a shrine so that they could continue to invigorate the ground. The local agencies of such "kindred spirits" were followed into the larger-scale contexts of the response to signs of decreasing fertility and increasing sickness in the linked people/ground domain. The basis of these rituals lay in the idea that the ancestors were those who held the key to the restimulation of fertility. In one part of a major ritual, the Liru, male participants fed banana juice to the skulls of prominent leaders of the past, in order to gain the ancestors' favor and help to renew the fertility of the land/kin group.

The perceived importance of the ancestors for the renewal of the world is marked by the narrations of descent that form the ideological frame-work for each parish (*rindi*). These narratives signify an unbroken chain of ties with the past, offering legitimization of occupation for the current generations and also a connection of power channeled through the genea-logical ties that can be tapped into by means of ritual. Although the form of descent applied to parish membership in general is cognatic, that is, can be traced through either male or female links, ideological precedence is accorded certain agnatic lines encompassing prominent males who were leaders in the parish. The "line of power" entailed thus runs through agnatic kin, producing a symbolic hierarchy among parish members and giving a responsibility to agnatic leaders to act as preservers of the parish's viabil-ity by making appropriate sacrifices to the ancestors and to the spiritual powers of the landscape at large. The leaders could then draw on the other group-members, including the wider cognatic category of kin, to raise the material resources needed for the sacrifices. The ecological correlate of this ritual imperative was that people would be stimulated to raise more pigs and plant more crops to feed them so that these could be in turn ritually invested in bringing about more fertility through sacrifice to ancestors. The closed circuit of ritual was thus fed by an open circuit of productive activ-ity, aimed at restoring the ecosystem to a state of prosperity and health. The implication is that ritual actions were woven in with productive actions in a nexus of people-environmental relations. In looking at ecological out-comes in any productive regimen we need to take into account such cycles of consequences of action, and how they contribute to or complicate issues of sustainability.

3   Arguments about the commons

It is clear from our Duna, Papua New Guinea, example that in order to understand its intricacies we need to be aware of how the Duna system of kinship and descent operated as an adaptive device in relation to the environment. The same point underlies conclusions from another area of study, first signaled in ecological writing as the "tragedy of the commons" (Hardin 1968). The basic argument here began from an image of separate, individual actors, each seeking to maximize returns on profit from their input of labor. In other words, it began with the classic *homo economicus* model of humans that informed orthodox economic theory at various times in the past. Such a homo, faced with competition for access to common upland grazing ground for animal stock, might be expected to keep as many stock animals as possible on the commons, and if the other users did the same, the resource could disappear. That is, without authoritative control over the grazing, this form of common property would become unsustainable.

Hardin's model for the supposed tragedy of the commons depended on him stripping away from it any cultural or social values adhered to by stockkeepers and replacing these, as we have noted, with a set of assumptions about how people would behave in some circumstances of stress or competition over resources. Hardin took his beginning from a much earlier work, dating to 1833, by a mathematician called William Forster Lloyd (Hardin 1968: 28). Following the argument of Lloyd, Hardin develops his pastoral *mise en scène*. He does not direct his readers to any previous ethnographic sources, but he tells us to "picture a pasture open to all". That is, an "unlimited commons", with no existing social rules governing its use. Hardin next asserts that every herder will try to graze as many cattle as they can on this shared common land. So long as circumstances would keep the numbers of people and animals below the land's "carrying capacity" (Hardin, p. 29) no crisis would occur, he says. (The definition of "carrying capacity" might require consideration here, with some implication of ecosystemic sustainability.)

Hardin builds in his next assumption that each herder is "a rational being" (p. 29) and will therefore try to maximize his gains. (No mention of social units or gender here—just male individuals.) Such a herder will add at least one animal to his stock if he can, and Hardin assumes he will do so in order to make a gain by selling it. (However, pastoralists do not necessarily keep animals for sale.) The net effect may be that the area becomes overgrazed, but this will not deter each individual from their chosen path to increase their herd. Hardin further says that each herder will keep on increasing his herd until all the herders are ruined. He concludes, "Freedom in a commons brings ruin to all" (p. 29).

Hardin provides a number of examples where such freedoms lead to trouble, and one example is quite telling. He points out how the indiscriminate dumping of waste and the pollution of the environment can be seen as an example of the misuse of the commons. This is quite correct, and the global problem of waste is much bigger now than it was when Hardin wrote this essay (see, for example, Eriksen 2016). Hardin also points ,quite correctly, to population problems in the world—again, much greater today than in 1968—and he adds that if the freedom to breed is treated as a kind of commons the world will also be locked "into a tragic course of action" (p. 31), via unsustainable levels of population. Hardin advocates private property rather than the commons and notes that coercion is needed to control people's behavior.

It is easy enough to understand why Hardin's argument might be considered compelling and important. But its flaw is that it starts from assumptions rather than facts. The herder he invokes is not a herder such as those among the Nuer people of South Sudan, at least in earlier times when the social anthropologist Edward Evans-Pritchard made a detailed study of this area (Evans-Pritchard 1940). The Nuer were predominantly pastoralists, with herds of cattle, seeking pastures in different areas according to season, and with a complexity of tribal social structure that guided their choices of where to drive their cattle and when to plant crops of maize to supplement their diet. While conflicts could occur, the Nuer had intricate ways of managing pasture areas for their animals.

In discussing how "the commons" works as a concept we have to be careful about definitions. Hardin's concept set the direction for this whole analysis: a pasture "open to all". This is only one type of situation. A very detailed book on common field usages in historical England begins with a more circumscribed definition, as follows: "A common field is one in which various parts or parcels of land (or the use of them) belong to individual proprietors, who exercise sole proprietary rights when the land is in crop but leave them in abeyance when it is not" (Kerridge 1992: 1).

This is a very particular definition, completely different from Hardin's. It is also quite unlike the situation of the Nuer people and their transhumant practices of moving their herds about in search of pasture. Kerridge notes that "hundreds of years ago common fields were a familiar part of the English landscape" (p. 1), and that while they do not any longer exist there they are commonly found in parts of Europe: a situation that continues to exist today. Temporary fences may mark off one plot from another, but common fields are not permanently enclosed or bounded. In the English common fields various methods of ploughing were employed and trenching to remove water from the field and dispose of it in ditches was required. Not all fields were ploughed. There were heaths and hills and permanent meadows (Kerridge, p. 12), also known as leys (p. 15). Such permanent common meadows were kept in grass and were not to be ploughed for cultivation, unless by general consent. In ploughed fields, Kerridge notes (p. 11), the maintenance of drainage was overseen by officials called "haywards". Balks between cultivated plots separated the plots and provided grass for pastures (p. 13). Common lands for tillage or pasture go back a long way, to Anglo-Saxon times, in the tenth century CE Common fields also had to have farmyard manure spread on them or contained sheep folds with hundreds of sheep for each common proprietor (Kerridge, pp. 26-27), and all this would be done "according to strict regulations" (p. 27). Folds of this kind for animals held in common, Kerridge points out, constituted the reason "compelling the common management of intermixed and intermingled parcels" (p. 34).

In addition, the parcels themselves came into being at least partly as a result of co-heirs obtaining pieces of land over the generations, and this, in turn, implies that such co-parceners would be related by kinship and thus able to co-operate on the basis of such ties. This factor does not appear in Kerridge's account, because he is not thinking in terms of kinship groups and norms but, rather, in technical and material terms relating to practices of ploughing the land, headlands, ditches, and perimeter markers. Our summary here of his account does, however, make it abundantly clear that the pattern of "the commons", which he delineates is a far cry from the model articulated by Garrett Hardin. It is relevant here to note that common fields were often mixed in with fields held under different arrangements, and special agreements had to be negotiated in order to regulate fallowing or fencing (Kerridge, p. 33). At a later stage again, common field systems began to disappear when parcels of land became consolidated "into large blocks and flocks in the hands of capital farmers" (p. 42). Here, then, a different story begins. For one thing, with the growth of enclosures of land in private ownership, regulations of remaining common fields tended to lapse. To counter this process in turn, an official Act of 1773 allowed farmers to elect officials called "reeves" to enforce rules passed previously in collective town hall meetings (p. 73).

Kerridge makes occasional mention of situations in Scotland and Ireland, where there was a pervasive division between in-fields, mostly cultivated, and out-fields, used for common pasture. The blocks of fields in Scotland were called runrigs (rundales in Ireland). Out-fields supplied extensive rough pasturage for stock, and in-fields provided the crops of barley, oats, and turnips, or hay for the wintering of animals. From the middle of the eighteenth century until the turn of the twentieth century, exercise of rights over land by the small-scale tenants of lairds, or landlords, was progressively undermined by enclosures of land and evictions of the tenants.

The tenants had lived in fermtouns, clusters of families congregated close to the runrig strip that they cropped (see, for example, Gray 2010). A subclass of people, the cottars, lived on small patches of land in conditions of precarity, and in places accounted for two-thirds of the rural population (Aitchison and Cassell 2012: 23). It was these cottars who suffered most from the "improvements" of the eighteenth-century lairds (landowners), because they had no legal rights and could easily be removed. By contrast, single family tenants could have an oral or written lease agreement, with some expectation of continuing, and an understanding of an ongoing business relationship with their laird. Rent now came to be paid in money rather than in crops or dairy produce. On the Borders, landlords began to enclose land in order to raise cattle for export to England, squeezing out cottars. In Galloway, there was a resistance movement against these enclosures, but it was forcibly put down and its supporters were imprisoned or were banished and emigrated overseas. Some aristocratic landowners proceeded in Berwickshire to appropriate large tracts of common land, and to drain this land, fertilizing it with lime, and adopting new crops and rotations from England. Towns grew in size, requiring their inhabitants to be fed. Tenants who could supply this food prospered (Aitchison and Cassell 2012: 56) Landlords, in turn, increased the rent rates. In the towns new industries developed. On the land estates, the owners came to rely on the work of managers known as factors to implement the changes of agricultural practices associated with increases in income and rents.

These "improvements" in agriculture prefigured a continuing process that is still reflected today. Did these improvements increase or decrease the sustainability of the agricultural system? The old runrig system had lasted for a long time and was from this perspective sustainable. However, once opportunities and constraints relating to development emerged and generated new ambitions of the landowning class, the old system became vulnerable and indeed unsustainable. The human cost, however, of the innovations has to be taken into account. Sustainability of the new system went hand in hand with an unsustainability of the old ways. So sustainability is in the eye of the beholder. Today, farmers in Scotland still work hard to remain in business and competition in a highly commoditized context, complicated further by the UK's planned withdrawal from the European Union and uncertainties over the future continuation of government subsidies for farmers.

From where we began this discussion, on Hardin's model of the tragedy of the commons, it has been clear that the elements he built into his model do not apply in the cases we have explored here. In England complex regulations and arrangements maintained common fields until the system changed in the direction of private property holding and profit-oriented economics. A comparable process took place in Scotland, but a further element emerged, which we could reasonably call "the Tragedy of the destruction of the commons" there, as a result of the sufferings endured by the poorest class of subtenants or cottars who were driven off their land by the processes of "improvement" instigated by landlords and their factors. We are faced again with the point that enhanced sustainability for the owners meant a loss of a former state of sustainability of the cottars.

The debate about the commons had a further considerable spin-off. Elinor Ostrom and her colleagues developed a whole new way of looking at how varieties of practices involving the use of resources held in common can contribute to the understanding and management of such resources (see, for example, Ostrom 1990, and detailed studies in Bardhan and Ray ed. 2008). The "common fields" of England, the runrigs of Scotland, and the rundales in Ireland, were all consciously managed human creations. At a wider level that has become relevant, global resources such as the atmosphere of our planet, or wildlife in forests and grasslands, or the state of oceans and the pollution of fish and other creatures in them, a set of issues arise that can be looked at in terms of theories of the commons. These are issues that cannot be addressed in Hardin's fashion by advocating a shift from "common" management to private ownership. Scott Barrett, a Professor of Natural Resource Economics at Columbia University, treats issues surrounding climate change as a new "tragedy of the commons" (Barrett 2018: 1217). In order to mitigate or reverse the effects of human-induced climate change, there would need to be an overall authority or nation-states would have to agree on, and follow, norms that could ameliorate these effects. These conditions have not yet been met, Barrett notes. Models of organization based on research finds about local commons are not easily transposable to a global level and the sustainability of life in general thus becomes moot. Ultimately, an overall shift in consciousness is needed in order to produce viable norms at this global level.

4   Traditional conservation
and cash-cropping in
Papua New Guinea

The debate on "the commons" is cognate with a general debate on whether gardening practices in pre-cash cropping contexts in places such as Papua New Guinea included practices of conservation or not. The issue is difficult to elucidate because observations tend to have been made when cash cropping had already been initiated along with other changes in politics, both in colonial and post-colonial times.

Today, population growth, mining, and agricultural intensification have all proceeded apace in Papua New Guinea (PNG). Both outside observers and indigenous people in various government or unofficial roles have expressed concern over issues to do with the environment, and this mix of concerns is very well represented in the proceedings of a conference organized by the Institute of Applied Social and Economic Research (IASER) in October 1980, five years after PNG achieved political independence from Australia in September 1975. The conference was reported in a monograph on "Traditional Conservation" practices, published in 1982 by IASER (Morauta, Pernetta, and Heaney 1982). The monograph contains 43 chapters, and 23 of the authors or co-authors in it are Papua New Guinean citizens or academics. It represents, therefore, a high level of interest in environmental issues in what was at that time a very new nation-state. Many chapters elucidate what is meant by traditional conservation. We give some examples here. Ralph Bulmer, who was the Foundation Professor of Anthropology at the new University of Papua New Guinea in Port Moresby, spent many years on fieldwork in the Kalam area of Madang Province. Bulmer's approach to the topic is cautious and wide-ranging (Bulmer 1982: 59–77). He points out that agriculture causes greater environmental transformations than hunting and gathering. Cultural taboos on the contingent use of forest resources for hunting, such as restrictions on the capturing of wild animals like marsupials, helped wild populations to maintain their numbers. In times before European contact was established, from the 1930s on, in the Highland interior of New Guinea, the tools used for cutting trees or clearing stands of grass were all stone axes, adzes or wooden knives. When European outsiders arrived and brought with them steel tools, the efficiency of land clearing was greatly speeded up, making it feasible to clear bigger areas for less labor input. More food production thus facilitated population growth, and in turn this would accentuate production itself, leading to a cycle of intensification. With shifting cultivation and long-fallow practices, activities of cutting into forest areas would lead to a reduction in diversity of the useful food products available from gathering resources there.

In spite of these observations, Bulmer is careful to make it clear that among the Kalam, the population with whom he did long-term fieldwork in the northern fringes of the Highlands, there was a great variety of plant and animal resources for food and for construction, and these could be largely self-sustaining as long as cash cropping did not take over from subsistence work. Many practices had an overall effect of conserving resources in a sustainable way, even if this was not their primary or overall aim. In the 1960s, when Bulmer was working there, the Kalam had only quite recently been brought under colonial administration by Australian government officers. There was little reason for them to be concerned about loss of forest, when there was a frontier of further forest available. However, whenever such forest areas became scarcer, different procedures emerged. In the Mount Hagen area, in an area known as Dei Council after the administration established local government councils there in the early 1960s, there was an area of forest in between the gardens and settlements of two clans belonging to different tribes (wider political units). One of the two clans had immigrated from a distant place, having been pushed out in warfare and seeking asylum. The other clan belonged to a group that had immigrated there much earlier and had also been given land on the basis of ties of kinship and marriage. The newly immigrant group members included one man who cut into the edge of the forest at the upper end of a sloping and not very fertile area of land, seeking a better crop of mixed vegetables as well as the staple sweet potato crop. Leaders from the other clan protested against this move and threatened to take action against what they saw as an intrusion into an area where they were accustomed to gather forest products. The garden remained, but further expansion was halted. Both sides here were short of forest areas, so neither side wished to colonize the land extensively. The process was largely self-managed, without any elaborate authority being exercised.

A feature that Bulmer also discussed was the burning of grassland areas. When forest is cleared, and land is subsequently fallowed, tall grasslands may develop and they are then burnt down to facilitate the capture of game. Large areas of anthropogenic grassland may result, and such areas may be kept in this way, rather than being re-cultivated, for the sake of periodic hunting. Land is thus lost from both forests and gardens over time and long-term grassland appears as a kind of disclimax growth, hard to bring back into cultivation.

In our own field experience, the practice of burning grassland came to our attention in another remote part of the Highlands, among the Duna people, during our stays in the 1990s. The grassland areas there were low-lying, in a valley near to the big Strickland River, a hot, dry area without gardens or dwelling houses but home to wild pigs. Hunting there was a kind of sport, but in the accident that had led to unfortunate results. Some hunters had set the grass on fire to drive out pigs, and the wind had turned the fire around, encircling them and resulting in some of them dying in the flames. Soon, a rumor emerged that the change in the wind had been caused by local witches who could take the form of pigs and lure the hunters to their deaths. Seen in another light, these deaths could be interpreted as warnings against an excessive use of fire. The grasslands near the Strickland River are looked on as places of spirits that can be dangerous. The river itself and its banks are spoken of as under the domain of a powerful and respected female spirit, who looks after wild creatures of the bush. This spirit entity was said to be upset by the appearance of tailings from a massive gold mine in the Enga area, from which effluent came down into the Strickland and turned its water red. This spirit's domain had been spoilt by the mine tailings. Burning the grasslands on the river's margins had also disrupted the balance of living things there. In any case, the deaths and the suspicions of witchcraft that followed sufficed to cause a cessation of hunting in the area for some time, with conservational effects. The contingent intersection of ideas about spirits, witchcraft, and the female spirit kept the grasslands in relative equilibrium.

Another approach to conservation questions in rural Papua New Guinea contexts has to do with soil conservation and problems of erosion of soil due to rainfall (Wood and Humphreys 1982:95–114). In places where there is very high annual rainfall, as among the Kaluli people, forest trees are left standing with crops growing under their canopy, and then the trees are felled over the crop, helping to retain the soil while still protecting vulnerable plants. Elsewhere in the Highlands, people make rough terraces of logs to hold soil on steep slopes. In the Hagen area, gridiron trenches in gardens or mounding of earth also helps water runoff. Soil fertility can be improved by burning rubbish so that it produces fertilizing material. Leaf mold can be placed in holes to help individual plants such as yams to grow. Among the Maring and others, for example Hagen, gardeners pull out herbaceous weeds to prevent grass growing and the gardeners protect tree seedlings. Where smaller mounds replace gridiron trenches in the Hagen area, larger mounds protect against high rainfall. Gridiron ditches are made where rainfall is constant but not heavy. Deeper ditches are made to carry away excess water in swampy areas. In the highest parts of the Highlands, where there is a large amount of forest, larger mounds have the added function of composting, along with ample drainage, to keep the soil warm.

Soil conservation is therefore a part of long-established gardening techniques, but as Wood and Humphreys point out, soil fertility does tend to drop over time with continuous use (Wood and Humphreys 1982), and notable population increases in the Highlands since the 1930s have intensified pressure on land resources. This pressure has been increased by two further factors. One is the use of land for the production of coffee, a process that began in earnest in the 1960s with encouragement for the indigenous farmers to turn over some of their more fertile subsistence land to this new crop. The other factor is the growth of towns and cities. At this time also larger tracts of indigenously owned land were being leased or sold for expatriate-owned plantations, so that large-scale and small-scale production of coffee existed side by side. Such tracts often were not under current cultivation and were lying in fallow or in swampy parts that needed to be drained, proving to be very fertile once this happened. The net effect overall was that much land was removed from actual or potential subsistence use and converted into commodity production. Money from coffee growing has to be used in pursuit of new needs for introduced forms of clothing and consumption of foods such as rice and fish or tinned meat, as well as more expensive things such as motor vehicles used to transport rural people to urban stores or to take vegetable produce to sell in town. Urbanization swallows up further areas of agricultural land, and places demands on roads and transport of goods, while providing a market outlet for people who still have access to land that is good for vegetables, if it is not entirely lost to long-term plantings of coffee. In addition, of course—and this is perhaps the biggest factor of all—since the 1930s there has been a steady growth in the population of PNG, at least partly domiciled in rural areas. This growth tends to be combined with the weakening of traditional practices of the spacing of children with lengthy post-partum taboos on sexual intercourse that were supported by the indigenous religious ideas and are undermined by the adoption of Christianity. Processes of independently precipitated change combine, therefore, to produce net ecological effects that increase pressure on resources and increase also dependence on the outside world to meet needs (see, for example, Stewart and Strathern 2002b, 2009; Strathern and Stewart 1999, 2000, 2007).

There is ample evidence, then, that numerous methods were employed by gardeners in the PNG Highlands to protect their subsistence crops and conserve the fertility of the soil on which these crops grew, either by ditching, mounding, or fallowing. When coffee as a cash crop entered the picture, new pressures on the land emerged.

In the northern part of the Mount Hagen area in PNG the Australian-run Department of Agriculture, Stock, and Fisheries first began promoting the cultivation of coffee by the indigenous Hagen people in the early 1960s, along with the introduction of Local Government Councils, communal road work, and the concept of paying Council tax as a way of supporting local development. All this was a part of a "modernization" project aimed at changing people's life patterns and steering them toward an economy based on money and commodities. Coffee was to lead the way into this new late-colonial world of money and commodities, and away from pigs and pearl shells, the prestigious items in the old exchange economy of the early-colonial times of the 1930s to the 1950s. Interestingly, at first Administration field officers encouraged the planting of communal plots of seedlings, from which individual growers would take plants for cultivation on individual plots. Such plots were established on ground held in fallow by a particular group, clan or subclan. Coffee seedlings require some protection in their early stages of growth and people would cover them over with knotted pieces of grass as hats for this purpose. They also planted banana trees, maize corn, cucumbers and the like, to assist in giving protection to the new crop.

The phase of communal seed-beds was temporary, like fallow land that can be viewed as a kind of "commons" until it is cleared again for planting. At that time, one or two men would usually open up a plot on ground previously used by their kinsfolk, typically their fathers. The new coffee seedling plots were established in a similar way, but without clear understanding of who was to be responsible for their ongoing maintenance. Administration officers made periodic inspections and gave advice in cultivation, but it was not possible to prevent theft of seedlings or damage to them by pigs. After small pockets or plantations were established by individual farmers and their families, coffee began to spread over the hillsides, appearing in all the settlements and often planted immediately around the dwelling houses where the owners could watch over and protect them against theft.

The type of coffee tree that flourished in the Highlands of PNG was, and is, Arabica. James Sinclair notes (1995:4) that Arabica coffee suits the Highlands and Robusta the Lowland regions of PNG. Arabica accounts for over 80% of the coffee grown in PNG and the tree produces "mild, high quality coffee" (ibid.). The trees require pruning to keep them in a shape suitable for harvesting. They start to bear their berries about three or four years after planting. They can last fifteen years or more, and Sinclair notes (p. 5) that at the time he was writing (1995 was the publication date of his book) some trees that were planted thirty or forty years ago were still bearing. Today (2018 and 2019) it is unlikely that they would still be in production. Coffee plantations therefore have to be renewed by removing old trees and planting new ones. This is the first issue of sustainability, easily observable by planned replanting. Coffee trees are also susceptible to coffee rust disease (Sinclair 1995: 384–402).

Sinclair's account makes it abundantly clear how important the coffee industry became in Papua New Guinea, especially the Highlands, both to plantation owners and to small-scale producers. The plantation owners were initially expatriates from Australia, often closely linked in with government officials and often also having long-term commitments to Papua New Guinea. Later, with government sponsorship, many plantations were taken over by indigenous groups, notably the Pipilika corporation in the Western Highlands Province. In Dei Council, the highly productive Tiki plantation in the Baiyer River Valley was purchased by the Local Government Council from the widow of the entrepreneur John Collins, who had been related to the Leahy family. Plantations had required capital to establish and a supply of local labor to maintain them. Small-scale production increased rapidly, and after a while equaled, or overtook, the plantation sector in productive capacity. Both sectors were seriously threatened in the mid-1980s by the discovery of the coffee rust disease in smallholder coffee plots near to the Tiki plantation. This is a very serious disease that could wipe out the sustainability of the whole coffee industry on which the Highlands region greatly depended. Such a crisis is typical in monocrop commodity regions. With the heavy involvement of indigenous farmers in the industry, the issue was also palpably political, as the Prime Minster of the day, Paias Wingti, realized. Much of his support came from coffee industry stakeholders. He would face re-election in 1987. Other prominent locals were lining up against him.

In order to control the outbreak, coffee buying was suspended, trucks were fumigated, and a huge amount of spraying equipment was sent by Australia to Mount Hagen for immediate use. The Australian government continued to assist with a laboratory and spray workshop (Sinclair 1995: 397). Officers from the Queensland Department of Primary Industry, acting as consultants, appointed two experts, Mick Belfield and Dave Willis, to oversee the capabilities of local official bodies to handle the coffee rust.

These two officers held numerous training camps for extension field officers and visited many coffee growers where the trees were sick and not pruned properly. They managed to re-establish viable small-holdings and to install spraying programs for rust disease control. In this way, the sustainability of the coffee economy was preserved.

Coffee remains important today in the Highlands, but there are many international competitors (see West 2012 for a detailed discussion of the growing and marketing of this crop in the Highlands of Papua New Guinea). There were official efforts in 2019 to revive the coffee industry, and on a visit in that year to the Jiwaka province east of Mount Hagen it was evident to us that there were many flourishing coffee plantations previously established by expatriate entrepreneurs and now taken over by indigenous groups and individuals.

In our recent visits to the Highlands in 2018 and 2019, we noticed a number of further changes. First, many of the plantations originally established by expatriate owners in the Western Highlands Province had fallen into disuse, partly as a result of intractable and violent disputes among the original landowners after they were taken over and returned to indigenous control. Second, old coffee trees that were not pruned or fertilized, were dying back after a span of some twenty years. Third, local growers were turning to the market production of fresh vegetables to feed a burgeoning urban population in Mount Hagen city.

In other words, the coffee-based economy had reached another hazardous point of reduced sustainability. In general, sustainability is a product of history and is therefore mutable, depending on changing economic factors as well as overall ecological effects, such as the age of trees, their management, and fluctuating soil fertility. An interesting comparison can be found with the relatively recent development of a new coffee industry run by indigenous groups in southern Taiwan. During the time of Japanese control in Taiwan of 1895–1945, the Japanese planted some coffee trees in mountainous locations belonging traditionally to indigenous groups. They did so not to establish an industry for these groups, but for their own consumption. After the Japanese rule ended in 1945, the coffee fields were neglected for many years, until within the last ten years after Typhoon Morakot indigenous Paiwan were relocated away from the mountains into villages in flat country and were in need of some new kind of activity. Some went back to the old Japanese plantations and either began to prune and take care of the trees or took cuttings from them and established new plantings on plots of land beside their houses. The old trees that had survived were hardy stock and flourished, producing good coffee cherry, assisted by agricultural extension staff. Down in the relocation areas outlets were established to process the coffee, roast it, brand it and undertake to distribute it to urban outlets. This part was done with government help. The whole development was a surprising creative response to the challenges of resettlement, and it gave the relocated villagers a new sense of identity, thus contributing notably to the sustainability of village enterprises.

5   Mining and its effects in Papua New Guinea

Large-scale mining enterprises have been important in Papua New Guinea since colonial times. Indeed, the earliest explorations of the central highlands regions by the Leahy brothers took place because of a search for gold deposits in highland streams at the fast-flowing headwaters of rivers, for example, Kuta south of Mount Hagen where Danny Leahy established a mining and sluicing site in the 1930s. The sluicing operation continued there until 1953. One of the effects of Leahy's enterprise was that he paid the local people with shell valuables for their laboring work, thereby altering the forms of circulation of wealth and the acquisition of status. Danny Leahy was to pay one pearl shell for about a month's work, or four or five cowrie shells per day, raised to ten later. About a dozen small nassa shells would purchase as many pounds of sweet potatoes, a staple food (A. Strathern 2007, orig. ed. 1971: 104). Funneling these shells into local exchange circuits fundamentally altered the distribution of goods and the parameters of power in the Hagen society. Although the overall effects on the physical environment were minor, the social effects of introducing shell-wealth into Hagen were considerable, and this would have triggered longer term alterations on exchange rates and ways of exercising control.

The Leahy brothers also were associated with the Australian administration's field officer, James Taylor. In one exploratory patrol in 1938, the Hagen-Sepik Patrol. Taylor led a party far into what later became the Enga Province of Papua New Guinea; and he subsequently established a gold property license at Porgera. Porgera later became the site of a huge gold and copper mine, dwarfing Taylor's original claim where he had sluiced for gold in old-fashioned pans with a small number of workers.

Taylor's old claim sits curiously as a forerunner of two very different projects. One of these became the giant Porgera mine, which we will discuss later. The other is known as the short-lived Mount Kare "gold rush". Mount Kare is a remote rugged mountain notable for its karst limestone rocks and high-altitude swamp area, *Kare Puga*. As Peter Ryan remarks

in his book about the discovery of gold in Kare, indigenous people neither knew about the presence of gold in their land nor would they have
valued it if they did. The area lies at above 9,000 ft asl, is riddled with
sinkholes into which rivers disappear, and has no road access. In the 1980s
CRA Exploration Pty. Ltd. took over a prospecting lease previously held
by Placer Development and its geologists began surveying and assessing
the area, looking for alluvial gold in riverbeds, colluvial gold located in
the debris from landslides, and pockets of gold veins to be found in rock
fissures exposed by weathering. They closed their camp over Christmas
1987, and when they returned in February 1988 they found that indigenous
prospectors had occupied space along the Gewa River and were busy wash-
ing huge quantities of gold nuggets out of the mud and rock. The working
conditions were taxing and dangerous, but the returns were considerable.
Ryan (1991: 28) estimates that between 1988 and 1989, some 30 million
Kina of income was won from the ground by small-scale mining enterprises
at Mount Kare. The miners, who brought their own simple shovels, bush
knives, and pans, were also local landowners or connected to the owners by
cognatic kinship, so they were able to claim the right to engage in surface
activities of searching for gold. One problem was that the area spans the
Enga and Hela Provinces, with the potential for disputes between the Huli
people of Hela (or Southern Highlands as it was at the time) and the Engans
as to priorities of claims. Huli tribespeople had historical claims over the
gold-bearing places beside the Gewa River and the Kare Puga swamps, so
they quickly covered these areas with networks of claims, 20,000 or more
small pits occupied by at maximum 7,000 miners and their families (Ryan,
p. 49). A geographer, Professor Richard Jackson, estimated that in 1988 a
third of the adult males in the Paiela census district were away from their
villages mining for gold (Ryan, p. 50). Mount Kare itself lies within Enga
Province, but land claims stretched across the artificial Provincial divid-
ing line. On both sides, stories proliferated linking gold to narratives about
large snakes—narratives paralleled by a comparable genre of folktale that
spread out from the Porgera area where a huge international consortium had
developed an industrial gold and copper mine, sparking social and environmental problems going far beyond those generated by the Mount Kare
gold rush. The Mt. Kare episode was virtually over by the end of 1989. The
company CRA set up an arrangement for industrial mining in the area, in
collaboration with local people, but violence interposed itself with an attack
on the CRA mining camp, and CRA suspended its operations there. Ryan's
book closes on this note (p. 140).

Several factors were involved in determining the lack of sustainability
of the mining at Mount Kare. First, the whole area was formidably difficult to work in. Short-term gains offset this circumstance. When surface

digging had obtained what it could, the bonanza was over. The landscape gradually recovered. The miners spent their wealth. By contrast, the huge Porgera mine continues in operation, but it has also generated massive environmental results and social tensions with a long-term modification of the landscape and issues of pollution from tailings reaching as far as the great Strickland River that runs into the Fly river system, into which in turn flows the Ok Tedi, site of yet another massive gold and copper mine and associated environmental pollution.

The Ok Tedi mine is named after a big river that runs through its area and connects to the south with the Strickland River and Fly River. The mine is located quite close to the northern coast of Papua New Guinea. Areas to the north of the mine and areas immediately around it have had considerable resources for development poured into them since the mine was first established in the Mount Fubilan site. Gold production was begun in 1984, with removal of a "cap" of gold from the top parts of Mount Fubilan (Burton 1997: 36). A plan to set up a tailings dam to contain the outflow of tailings was curtailed by landslides, and there were two cyanide spills into the river systems, polluting drinking water supplies. The company, Ok Tedi Mining Ltd. (OTML) was permitted by the PNG government to release mine tailings and waste rock into the river, and amounts released went up by 1991–1995 to "more than 40 times what had been suggested in 1984" (Burton op. cit., p. 37). With this increase, flooding of the river emerged, dumping slurry wastes on people's gardening areas. Periodic dry conditions, heightened by the climatic fluctuations known as El Nino, trapped sediment upstream and masked the potential for flooding. In 1995–1996 severe flooding ensued with destruction of crops and vegetation dieback. Demands by the local people for compensation for environmental damage sprang up. Roadblocks accompanied these demands. The OTML Company put in place arrangements for the physical environment, but less was put into social monitoring. More community affairs staff were needed. International organizations were involved, for example, the German parliament called on the German shareholders in the mine to make better ways of disposing of mine tailings and of compensating the landowners, the Yonggom people, for damage done to their environments. At the provincial level there was dissatisfaction with the way money from the Development Grant from the national government was disbursed. Problems and issues of this kind form a recurrent feature of arguments in Papua New Guinea about the distributions of compensation funds for environmental damages and also for general services such as for health care. Studies of this problem for the Porgera mine, studies that were organized by the National Research Institute, have found that funds paid out by the mining company there (Porgera Joint Venture) to the national government do not find their way effectively to the local populations they are intended to assist. Contrariwise, monies intended to help communities with specific projects such as building a bridge or an aid post for health workers are sometimes said to be pocketed by individuals instead of being applied for collective benefit (see Filer 1997). Compensation therefore does not work well as a mechanism for settlement of grievances unless it is handled wisely, as the PNG government itself has at times recognized.

Another, related, matter emerged, who exactly should receive compensation? Two points are relevant here. First, OTML refused to pay compensation for trees or "unimproved land" used by the Company, a stance sensibly reversed by PJV in Porgera. Second, the national government, according to Filer (1997: 84), did not include as eligible for damages the people living downstream from the mine, by contrast with those living closer to it around in Tabubil. When severe pollution emerged in the downstream areas, it produced in the end a very large lawsuit and an out of court settlement in 1996 of US$500 million. How that money was to be distributed and accessed would be the next problem. Another process was set in hand in 2000 after the parent company of OTML, Broken Hill Proprietary (BHP), still did not keep to the requirement of controlling the mine tailings. BHP was required by a second settlement in 2004 to transfer its share in the mine to a development trust, but pollution of the river continued throughout these legal processes. BHP left the whole project in 2006, before the final settlement came into being.

The anthropologist who has done the most long-term committed study of one of the peoples most affected by the riverine pollution from the mine, the Yonggom of Dome village, Stuart Kirsch, documented in 1996 the massively ruinous effects of the mine tailings and sediment. His account goes well beyond immediate materialities, noting how memories of the environment and experiences in it are destroyed, causing mimyop, feelings of sorrow and loss, marked in sung laments (Kirsch 2014: 62)— which, we may suggest, are like laments for dead people that are commonly sung by women among the Duna people. Mining has destroyed an ecosystem that functioned for people as a commons resource (Kirsch 2014: 64). The mine's sustainability has undermined the sustainability of the landscape (ibid.).

Acid mine drainage increases the toxicity of the environment further, although OTML has produced a pipeline to send pyritic materials to a storage area. Confusion about the causes of pollution induced the Yonggom to talk about it as a form of sorcery (poison and sorcery are seen as interrelated), and this idiom was used by supporters of OTML to belittle the people's concerns (on ideas of witchcraft and sorcery in PNG see, Stewart and Strathern 2004). The state's depending on revenue from the mine reduced its capacity to monitor the mine's polluting effects. Kirsch aptly refers to the ensuing conflicts as a case of "colliding ecologies" (Kirsch 2014: 77). The cultural survival of the Yonggom was placed in jeopardy.

A striking feature of this whole history is the recalcitrance of the mining company to listen to or accede to the complaints of the people right up to the time when they were finally forced to pay out large sums of money. Numbers of research workers, prominently including Stuart Kirsch, had issued warnings that were conveyed to OTML managers, as well as to the outside world in general. Kirsch observes that the company and the government only began to take notice of such warnings when indigenous leaders took their case to international forums (Kirsch 2014: 85). The two most prominent leaders were Rex Dagi and Alex Maun. Both men had benefited from performing contract work for the company. These, and other, leaders were joined by a stream of concerned environmental NGO's and also by the Catholic Church in Kiunga. Company authorities began to argue that anthropologists were encouraging local resentments against the mine (Kirsch 2014: 98). But the anthropologists were merely bringing to light what indigenous villagers were saying. The mine authorities, however, did not budge, and Rex Dagi took them to court, seeking AUS$4 billion in compensation (Kirsch op. cit., p. 116). The writs included about 500 clan groups, totaling 30,000 people, joining the complaint. There was a huge and complicated struggle over the case. In the end, the plaintiffs won with an arrangement to include K40 million for the Yonggom and others of the lower Ok Tedi area. Subsequent to the case further problems arose about the agreement that the company would address the tailings pollution, and they in fact failed to do so. Despite the 1996 settlement and the subsequent one of 2014, OTML actually survived and was making a profit because of an increase in the prices of gold and copper, planning to keep the mine going for some more years.

How sustainable, then, was all this? Two conclusions can be drawn, in line with arguments presented in other parts of this book. The first is that sustainability at one level may be sacrificed to or compromised by sustainability at another level. In this case, the sustainability of the Papua New Guinea state depended on revenues from the mine. The mining company and its shareholders depended on income in order to turn a profit and to pay back investors. Major contentions with the local and downstream populations occurred from the company's disposal of tailings. The pumping of waste into the Ok Tedi river in turn destroyed the form and the sustainability of riverine ecological life-worlds of the indigenous people. Even with monetary compensation payments, the habitats in question could not really be restored. Eventually a large settlement was obtained from the parent company though litigation. The company, however, sustained its operations because of a rise in the price of gold and copper, without meeting all its obligations on waste disposed. The environment, and the indigenous people whose livelihood was bound up with it, comes out as a net loser. Life, as the Yonggom people had earlier created it, was rendered unsustainable, while the sustainability of the mine's global business networks was maintained. A comparative study of the large Porgera mine in Enga Province would show many comparable problems and issues but with better study and management of environmental issues and without such massive riverine damage. The comparison, then, would indicate that the stark conditions engendered by OTML in Ok Tedi were not inevitable and could have been avoided or at least mitigated.

6   Energy

Everything depends on supplies of energy, ways of creating, maintaining or boosting power. Entropy in systems signifies loss of power. The human body and brain require nutrients for conversion into energy on a regular repetitive basis, otherwise they will die. Water is an essential element for living creatures, and dehydration can lead to death. All the resources on which life depends must be renewable, in the sense that otherwise those dependent on them would also die. Only in the limiting case where a resource is apparently limitless, would this not be true. In some past times the attitudes of humans toward their environment perhaps veered toward practice based on assumptions of unlimited access to energy. There is little doubt that assumptions about limitless available resources for human life were fueled in the age of empire by ceaseless exploration, discovery, and subjugation of indigenous people by immigrant invaders. The incumbent globalized world system has arisen out of these assumptions. But everywhere limits are now recognized. The reason why concern for the environment and its sustainability has come to the fore, however, is not simply a fear of limited resources, but is based on the facts of human-induced environmental pollution which is dangerous to human life everywhere. Indeed, the more resources of a particular kind, for example coal, are available and used, the greater is the danger. The race for resources, then, carries with it a concomitant threat of extinction unless technological solutions are found. On the one hand, there is a growing demand for increased production of goods and commodities in order to meet the needs of increasing populations and their propensity to live in expensive energy-needy cities. On the other hand, such an increase, spread globally and encroaching everywhere, also threatens pollution of many kinds, thus potentially making our planet unable to meet such energy demands without collapse.

In this context, three efforts emerge. One is to increase the efficiency of food production. Success with this teaches people to continue reproduction rates, and also economic systems have to date needed more people as workers for production. Robots can do most tasks, and they do not have the same range of needs as humans, but they require advanced technology and high maintenance by comparison with humans. The second effort has to do with technology itself. Designers increase the use of technology to improve the design of machinery and make it more energy efficient. Such design work, however, is itself expensive. Third, efforts are made directly to reduce pollution, or to spread the effects of it by means of exchanges between countries. Countries also enter into agreements to reduce carbon-emissions and meet targets. This is where two intertwined ideas emerge: clean energy and renewable energy. These are separate concepts, but in practice they are usually combined, and in general exclude the use of fossil fuels that have supported development to date and continue to motivate searches for such fuels and materials across the world. The assumption here is that fossil fuels are neither clean nor renewable and are in addition very dangerous when used to produce nuclear power sources. The argument extends in various directions. Electric power is proposed for automobiles (and aircrafts) because it is cleaner than petroleum or diesel, and can be made reasonably practical, or in conjunction with a conventional motor. Fuel cells are another technological possibility that are being experimented with. Discussions then move on to how electricity itself is produced, and here forms of energy that are seen as both clean and as renewable are brought into play. In this context, solar power, wave power, and wind power sources are being developed. In Scotland there has understandably been an emphasis on wind power from turbines, although wave power is also being actively explored.

Since the Scottish National Party first came into power in the devolved administration of Scottish affairs within the Scottish Assembly, the emphasis on wind power has increased, some saying that this emphasis was created by Alex Salmond, who was at the time First Minister in the Scottish Assembly. In any case the aim has been to foster renewable energy sources as a part of a progressive environmental policy. Wind, water, and sun are not just "renewable", they are available all the time without any human action. Of course, to turn them into usable energy in the form of electricity does require a considerable technological input. So, the idea is that these sources of energy should at any rate not cause environmental pollution. There are other logistic concerns, however. Among these is the question of the cost of different types of energy, in monetary terms and in other ways also.

Wind turbines are very large, standing high over the countryside. Close up, they make a strong swishing sound that can be disturbing to the human ear, and possibly also to animals such as sheep that may be kept on upland mountain pastures where the turbines are also situated. The turbines must be kept a certain distance away from human dwelling space, and this generally means that they are constructed on remote heaths and hill slopes. Installing them requires access for very large trucks that carry their components including their massive blades. Roads may have to be widened to enable such installation, running through small villages on the way. In one case, near to the village of Alyth in Perthshire, Scotland, a large scheme was developed on a hill area, Drumderg, accessed by tiny roads. Because of the obvious inconvenience to the villagers, including road damage and hazards caused by the transport of parts, the villagers were offered forms of compensation by way of improved local amenities, which they accepted.

Developers also often have to deal with farmers on whose land the turbines are installed. Different farmers may own or work different portions of a mountain gazetted for turbines. The company that is involved can negotiate separately with each farmer for permission to go ahead and make a deal for this, usually a share of the income that each turbine generates. One farmer might feel less inclined to permit the development, but if others around consent, that farmer will become isolated and less able to refuse. Turbines generally require large amounts of space and also internal roads for access to the maintenance and checking of machines. The clusters of turbines can be small in number but more usually they are large, up to hundreds of individual turbines covering wide areas of landscape, such as in Whitelee in northern Ayrshire in Scotland. In the case of such a large area, disruption to the patterns of movement of wildlife can be considerable, so that a whole complex ecosystem is altered.

For humans the noise pollution and the perceived negative effects on the landscape emerge as the major factors of concern. Noise arises as an issue only if turbines are nearby. But another element of analysis enters when we take into account perceived effects of turbines on the well-being of the local people. Theorists of sustainability have now begun to take the notion of well-being into account in their analysis. In one northern Scottish area, one category of villagers strongly opposed a turbine proposal while another category firmly supported it. The conflict threatened the well-being of both sides. Those who wanted the proposal to be put into effect tended to be poorer and to appreciate the material benefits the scheme would generate. Those who opposed it tended to be richer and to be offended by the appearance and noise of the turbines within sight of their dwellings. Local area inhabitants have to be consulted in public meetings and their agreements sought before a scheme can go ahead. Such meetings become an arena in which disagreement and dissent on class lines and perceptions of advantage and disadvantage arise, and these may be hard to resolve. The community may be consulted, but it may then show its character of disunity rather than unity. At issue is different perceptions of well-being, separately from sustainability *sensu stricto*.

A serious case of such disagreement arose in a different case, in South Ayrshire, in the village of Straiton, which we visited in 2017. Straiton is a picturesque village, with small shops, a pub, and access to striking mountain paths on numbers of sites around it. It has depended on its attractive location for tourists to come and spend their money. A plan to populate the scenic hills with massive wind turbines threatened the viability of the village economy based on tourism. This situation is the reverse of our previous example. In this, some people, for economic reasons, wanted the wind turbines to come in. In the present example, also for economic reasons, villagers opposed the schemes. Landscape aesthetics were also involved in both cases. In one, some people opposed the turbines for aesthetic reasons. In the second case, the same aesthetic concerns were raised but were linked to economics via tourism.

The case of Straiton village is of particular interest because there the village people organized themselves into an effective lobbying group to oppose the wind farm projects (see "Save Straiton for Scotland: Protecting Straiton, Neighboring Communities and Surrounding Countryside" webpage). We take here some information from records of the meetings of the "Save Straiton for Scotland", posted on "Visit Straiton". The coordinator at the meeting of March 3, 2019, reported that from 2013 onward they had fought to oppose six different wind farm projects, and had defeated five of these, the last one to be withdrawn being Linfairn. One that was too far advanced to be stopped by the time they began their campaign was Dersalloch, which had been started in 2007. A total of 92.6% of Straiton residents objected to the proposal by Scottish Power, and 4,723 people lodged objections, but it went through without a public inquiry. The Straiton group was invited to take part in a public inquiry into another project, Kiers Hill. They were keeping a watching brief on movements by the Scottish Power Renewables Authority that could indicate an intention to set up another wind farm scheme at Linfern Loch. They noted that gold mining proposals had been made in relation to the local forest park area, and they expressed their support for the idea of the Galloway National Park.

The group posted records of its struggles from February 2013 to 2019. The posting of July 21, 2018, recorded their battle over Linfairn. They had lodged an objection to the proposal, indicating that the turbines would be too noisy to be tolerated by the local people and would cause light shadow flickers. They had also objected in general that the scheme would damage the broader landscape and local ecology and would be too close to neighboring houses of Straiton families. They were assisted in their cause by many outsiders from numbers of countries who offered their support, and they relied on donations to finance their fight. Another posting, of November 26, 2017, noted that an extension of an existing windfarm at Handyard Hill had been turned down with a recommendation of refusal from the South Ayrshire County Council Planning Committee. In cases where the sonic effects are cited, it is considered that very low-frequency infrasound emissions are responsible for negative health consequences. These emissions are not audible and so people are not consciously aware of them, but they can have debilitating effects. Windfarm installations can also harm water supplies, as happened at the huge Whitelee project in Ayrshire, necessitating a costly replacement pipeline to be put in place. The group also mounted objections to further proposals for example Knockshae, Glenmount, and Kiers Hill. In all cases, complicated procedures had to be gone through, with ultimate decisions taken by government ministers after a public land inquiry, local representations, and recommendations at the county planning level. In a further case, relating to a site in Wigtown Bay, the official holder of the inquiry noted that the developers claimed renewable energy benefits for their project, but it was deemed that these were outweighed by the adverse impacts on landscape. Projects may also lower house price values, and they may infringe on the habitats of a variety of species, such as otters, bats, hen harriers, red squirrels and pine martens.

For all these communities, a further issue is involved. The turbines require to be replaced after 15–20 years, thus involving a second round of expensive transport and inconvenience all over again for the local people. In few, if any cases, has this happened so far in Scotland, but it is a part of the whole equation. A turbine therefore has a relatively short sustainable life and has to be replaced over time. Turbines are, however, renewable and do not pollute the air as coal-fuel plants do. They do "pollute' the landscape from the viewpoints of some people and may be dangerous to some categories of wildlife. Regulations restrict their location to sites not occupied by protected species. The cost of the electricity they generate has been brought down by technological advances. Individual landowners who operate turbines and produce a surplus beyond their own needs can supply the surplus to the national grid if the technology is right and a price agreed upon. Turbines can also be anchored strongly enough to situate them out at sea where they would not readily intrude on people's views. This is done on a large scale, for example, in the Netherlands, and a large scheme in the north of Scotland, opened in August 2019 by Prince Charles.

An example of a stark case of a conflict over the siting of a particular turbine took place on a farm worked by the tenant of a local estate at Glamis near Forfar in Angus County, Scotland. Here the turbine was to be sited rather near to the farm steading, and the farmer opposed this. The estate authorities, however, pressed ahead with the scheme. We heard about the case on a number of field visits while it was unresolved. The estate factor (manager) brought some pressure to bear via increased rent estimates.

The farmer eventually agreed. The case contrasts with another case where just a single turbine was to be installed. There the farmer owned the land. He established a turbine that directly overlooks the nearby village of Catrine in Ayrshire in Scotland. Locals grumbled mildly about it, but they became used to its presence high on the hill slope just north of the village. It is also just a single turbine, not part of a larger set such as at Whitelee. The farmer was also at the time on the local government council, which helped him to orchestrate support for his turbine. A more typical case pertains to a local farmer near to the village of Galston, north of Sorn in Scotland. Here one farmer whom we have known for many years owns land that has been used by a company for wind turbines. The farmer gets rent payments for the use of his land. Moreover, his wife was able to earn money for providing a place of construction workers to stay. Only a few turbines encroached on his immediate steading, but further away in a somewhat rundown neighboring farm that he owned, numerous turbines clustered round the steading and beyond it. The steading itself was in partial disrepair, with the roof off one of the structures. The farmland consisted largely of rough pasture, not capable of generating much income, so the turbines would bring in much-needed income. Indeed, this is probably a major factor in the siting of these wind farms, being placed on high altitude mountain slopes carrying only small numbers of stock and not too close to large populations of people. This feature explains why these wind farm projects are generally accepted by local communities. However, this same feature is the reason why in some cases there is community opposition. The remote hill areas are often ones that are important as attractions for visitors, who contribute to the local economy by paying for meals, accommodation, fuel, and sundry other expenses when they pass through, and as we have noted above visitors tend to appreciate unspoiled vistas of mountains and forests, without large swishing turbines intervening and sometimes complicating the possibilities for hiking in these areas. Even if there is provision for walkways, the experience of walking among turbines, or cycling around them, cannot be the same as walking in a genuine wilderness context. There is also another consideration. It is not only humans who are impacted by wind turbine installations, especially when these are large and cover considerable areas. Numbers of other species may be involved. Their movements may be impacted. They may run afoul of the actual turbines. Their breeding patterns may be disturbed. In certain cases, if rare or endangered species are placed at risk, a project to establish turbines may therefore not be approved by government authorities.

In terms of issues of sustainability, wind turbines offer clean energy and therefore contribute to environmental sustainability, in the same way as do solar power projects, for example. But their total cost for the consumers by comparison with fossil fuel sources such as coal has also to be taken into account. Solar power is more flexible, however, than wind turbines because it can work on very small or very large scales, and panels can be set up in ordinary fields in place of food crops, as we have seen in parts of Germany, or simply on rooftops of houses, as well as in huge sunny desert regions of the United States and China where otherwise few other activities could take place (certainly not tourism). Solar panels, like wind turbines, do require a complicated manufacturing process, including scarce materials, so we cannot ignore this factor in assessing the overall viability of these categories of energy production. Solar panels, however, are growing in popularity in many parts of Europe, and unlike wind turbines they are not sited in places of striking natural beauty nor are they visible from afar, any more than the crop tunnels that are used for fruit growing in Scotland and elsewhere. They are therefore relatively unobtrusive and can easily be shielded from view by natural cover. They do require regular maintenance by workers, and in China where such large schemes have been implemented in sunny desert or arid conditions persons who have been moved out of these areas have been relocated, trained, and employed to look after the panels in this way.

7 Farming, sustainability, and kinship

Sustainability depends greatly on community circumstances. While we have made this clear in reference to issues in places like Papua New Guinea, where kinship relations remain self-evidently an important part of life, we want in this chapter to argue that community relations are also important in industrial and post-industrial contexts, so that the sustainability of economic enterprises depends not only on technology and economic capital input but also on the social capital that springs from social relations. Studies of sustainability tend to lay stress on the physical environment, but the social environment is also important. Indeed, the two impact and influence each other. Ecology affects the way people organize their lives, and people's ways in turn have effects on ecology.

One way in which these processes are observable in advanced agricultural systems devoted to commodity production and the pursuit of profit lies within the spheres of network relations and problems of entry into and succession to property. Ecological conditions are also strongly inflected by the policies of government and further by the fluctuations of international trade, as well as by the hazards of disease of crops such as coffee. Environmental concerns have formed a focus of European Union policies in this arena, expressed in its agricultural regulations, enshrined in its policies for the support of agriculture applied throughout the EU. Recognizing the unique historical importance of agriculture as one of the foundations of rural life, EU policies have intersected with farming concerns in a number of ways: by providing conditions that assist in the welfare and supply of services to rural communities, including the farming sector but not restricted to them; by giving direct support payments as subsidies to farmers according to the size of their holdings; and by giving incentives to farmers to follow land-use practices that encourage biodiversity and conservation of wild species. The details of this common agricultural policy have varied over time, with an initial situation calibrated according to the putative heads of stock animals on pasture or the crops harvested in arable fields, replaced in 2003 by a flat payment per amount of land owned by particular farmers. The EU also regulates the amount of slurry that can be supplied as fertilizer in pasture fields and recommends constraint in numbers of stock to reduce carbon emissions. All reports and applications for funding have to be completed by the farmers online, requiring an up-to-date knowledge of the relevant technology, and the meeting of deadlines. As with all EU business, the system depends on an elaborate bureaucracy based in Brussels, although the payments are also passed through the hands of individual government ministries, and are sometimes held up by delays caused by the failure of official computer programs and resulting in considerable inconvenience or hardship for the farmers involved. At the individual level—and here is a first point of special interest—senior farmers were often not computer-literate, and would rely on younger kinsfolk to help them complete the lengthy forms required to qualify for available subsidies, classically a son who had been to an agricultural college and expected to eventually succeed to the ownership or tenancy of the farm, either on the death or the retirement of the father. Alternatively, they might have to pay a specialist firm to do this task, costing them an unwanted extra expenditure. We see here a theme found in circumstances of change around the world: formal or instituted arrangements are subsidized by informal ones, often from within the sphere of kinship or local community relations.

The basic reason given for the whole edifice of the CAP is in a sense cultural in character, although the surface form it takes is purely economic. The reason is that farming is recognized as an important component in the care and stewardship of the land, preventing it from becoming overgrown and uncared for, making sure that the environment is ordered. Farmers are also spread widely, ensuring that access to their places needs to be maintained. Farming is, in other words, an intrinsic ingredient of local life, and assisting it is seen as an act of conservation of that way of life. In the past, this would have been more observably true because farmers employed many local workers and day-hire laborers. With the advent of mechanical equipment replacing such laborers a new situation arises, in which family labor becomes more crucially important, and the farm as an enterprise becomes vulnerable to shortages of labor, especially at particular times of the year. With the rising costs of hiring labor, farmers and their families may tend to self-exploit with increasing workloads to keep up with needs.

This situation is particularly marked in smaller farms with lower overall production and less capital investment or income availability. It is also marked in areas classified as "Less Favorable", upland pasture areas that experience stresses from weather and lesser fertility. These are areas that the EU payments are particularly designed to support, and thus to enable the farmers in them to stay on the land. Such areas are found in various parts of County Donegal in Ireland, for example, the hillsides around the scenic Reelan River, which qualify for special payments and suffer when these are slow in coming and would suffer more if they were withdrawn. There is a big contrast here between such small undercapitalized farms mostly involved in rearing stock and hand labor and much larger dairy farms in parts of Ayrshire in Scotland or even larger grain producing farms in the south of England or farms on estates in Perthshire in Scotland. The CAP system operates in all of these contexts, and the overall effect is that the status quo of inequality between farms is maintained, while the smaller operations are maintained in a marginal state.

Smaller and larger farms alike are subject to the problem of intergenerational succession. This takes two forms. The first is a product of family norms that give precedence to a son as a successor but delay the time at which a son may enter into legal succession. Farming is not a job, it is a total way of life, and a senior man often wishes to remain actively involved in the work well beyond the notional retirement age for some other professions. There is also the point that in many ways a daughter could equally well be the successor if she wished this and were given the opportunity, rather than marrying into a farming family and joining a husband who is classified as the farmer, or else marrying out to continue with farming but want to train for some other profession and perhaps move away from their natal home. This may create an opportunity for someone else to purchase or rent the farm, perhaps a son of a farming family who because of the land going to an eldest son in the family cannot inherit it. This corresponds to the other facet of succession problems, that land does not regularly enter the market and so opportunities for younger people to enter into farming are restricted outside of inheritance. To ensure both continuity and revitalization of farming practices there is a recognized need to ameliorate this situation. A very big problem is that land prices are very high, and a young person may have abundant energy but not much money or collateral to offer in a loan application. All of these circumstances underline the point that the sustainability of a particular farm may be moot depending less on ecology and more on family dynamics.

Much can be gained in the context of such dynamics through partnerships of various kinds. A farmer may not wish to retire as yet but may be able to set up a child in another farm through a mortgage arrangement in which the original farm stands as collateral. The usual precipitating factor here is the junior generation's intent to marry and so to set up a new household and property unit.

An article by Peter Cush and Aine Macken-Walsh (2016) explores topics of the kind we have broached here in further detail, drawing their materials from Ireland. They take up the issue in EU policy of how best to achieve the continuity of farming in small-scale contexts, with particular reference to getting young persons into farming. The authors note (p. 1) that on average only 6% of the holders of farms in EU countries are listed as under the age of 35 (6.2% in Ireland). In Ireland, less than 1% of usable land is sold each year on the open market (p. 2), offering few opportunities for buyers. EU policy makers have taken the line that the need is to move older farmers out from their properties, so that younger ones can move in. Accordingly, they have developed early retirement schemes (ERSs) for farmers to retire between the ages of 55–64, provided they hand over all aspects of their farm property, they can receive a fixed term pension. However, as we have already noted in general above, a senior farmer does not tend to want to be removed entirely from his farm in this way. Another problem is that a younger man may not foresee sufficient income possibilities in agriculture as a full-time occupation. Or he may not be able by himself to qualify for farm extension services. Hence, the authors point out, the ERS idea is culturally not well suited and would be unlikely to succeed as a measure for bringing in new farmers. In fact, the basic mistake is that the scheme does not take into account the prevailing kinship structures and values in the rural society. There is a need to recognize the roles of both younger and senior members in farming families and networks. The authors consider the utility and potential value of joint farming ventures (JFVs) as ways of improving sustainability. They do recognize that farmers under 35 in the EU as a whole run bigger and more productive farms, but they add that in Ireland there is little difference in farm sizes between younger and older farmers. In addition, another survey suggested that in 2014 only 37% of farms in Ireland were found to be economically viable in themselves, while another 31% achieved viability by having off-farm supplementary income (p. 4). From our own observations in Scotland we can comment that this kind of off-farm income is often earned by a male farmer's wife, and it is used for basic food and clothing for the family. Whether conducted on- or off-farm, it is family labor that keeps farms going, enhanced not only by physical work but also by the senior persons' experience and knowledge of changing environmental conditions and the requirements of animal stock. Young people thus learn from older ones (p. 5). JFVs enable farmers to work together and increase the leisure time they can have. They often operate between an older farm holder and a younger prospective heir, with both parties able to draw income from the enterprise (p. 7). The process of succession is gradual and gives time for mutual adjustments. The arrangement overall helps to support a wide range of farmers and fosters the idea of inter-generational support that is a part of Irish rural culture and historical practice.

A complementary study was made in Scotland by Lee-Ann Sutherland and Rob R.F. Barton (2011). The study was sponsored by the EU, with the purpose of finding out cultural and social factors facilitating co-operative exchanges of equipment and labor among farmers. The study was undertaken in the Upper Deeside region of Northern Scotland, where marketing difficulties for beef and lamb meat were causing local stresses. The farming families in this area were long established and stable. Farmers reported that they share smaller pieces of equipment more readily than larger and more expensive ones, such as a tractor. These larger items could be shared among close kinsfolk but not with others, except perhaps in an emergency and only if relations were good. The risk of lending to non-kin was cited in this context, along with the point that if equipment was borrowed and then damaged this would lead to bad social relations (p. 240). Rather than taking such a risk, farmers would pay on a contractual basis for services. With regard to sharing labor, informants said that this was done only where this was feasible. One man said that he could perhaps help neighbors more now that his son had come home. Labor help is usually offered only in emergency as a mark of good relations, or in the context of a death in the family, or it is offered on a more regular basis seasonally, as for silage-making when there are needs for rapid harvesting and the machinery to do it is kept busy day and night when necessary. Sheep-shearing can also be shared, but some farmers preferred to pay for contract labor rather than rely on the uncertainties of reciprocity among neighbors. In more remote parts of the area farmers do not have close neighbors, and they are often themselves the sole source of their labor, so the occasional help from others can be vital for them. In general, the study showed that helping neighbors could be an important component of sustainability in farming, but a more comprehensive picture of kinship relations in the area would have given readers a better idea of how cohesive the community was and how succession to farm ownership operated to supply continuity and sustainability.

An overall point that emerges from our discussions in this chapter is that EU policies couched in purely economic terms are nevertheless entirely directed toward cultural ends: the maintenance of farming and its products and its role in shaping the countryside and the landscape into which it is set. It is cultural sustainability that is perceived to be at stake, although this cannot be achieved without economic viability. The problems here are essentially the same for larger and smaller farms. Large dairy farms for example depend on elaborate equipment and constant computerized monitoring by workers. The end product also has to be sold at a fair price to supermarkets, but these organizations act for their customers to try and keep down what they pay to the farmer or the milk marketing bodies. One enterprising farmer we know in Ayrshire in Scotland has started to process and sell his milk products directly to local customers, also embarking on a project to keep his farm organic and to use contemporary scientific knowledge of soil conservation by encouraging worms to inhabit it and increase its fertility. This farmer thought all this up by himself after he returned to take over the farm following the decease of his father from cancer and the decease or illness of his father's parents. The farm carries a famous name associated with the eighteenth-century Scottish poet Robert Burns, although Burns actually was a tenant in the next door farm (which had the same name), and our enterprising farmer has been able to tap into the immense prestige linked to the name of Burns to make his business better known.

Farmland offers alternatives in terms of its potential uses, as the above example shows. In County Donegal in the Republic of Ireland, a stock farm was repurposed after passing by inheritance into the hands of a couple who are conservationists and vegetarians with a keen interest in the observation and recording of wildlife. The couple planted numbers of the farm's fields with tree species that are indigenous to the Irish landscape, including sessile oaks and hazel trees. The trees are all planted out in neat rows in two separate plantations on either side of the original farm steading. They are trimmed from time to time, or lopped, and felled as necessary and cut into logs for sale or domestic use. Special types of wood are sold and used for craft productions. The undergrowth is carefully controlled, and invasive species are discouraged from proliferating. Bluebells flower in season among the trees, and pathways are maintained to guide walkers. Niches for kinds of wildlife are left undisturbed. Badgers and foxes find refuge areas there. The owners take daily walks to observe butterflies and birds, and at night trap moths and record their incidence. They take groups of interested people around to show them the plantations, and they give consultations to local farmers who express interest in conservation practices such as leaving some areas of land free from cultivation or keeping hedges for birds and small animals to inhabit, in return for EU subsidies. The husband is also employed on conservation assessment projects throughout Ireland, and they maintain an active network of like-minded people with environmental interests especially in County Donegal. The original farm steading buildings, previously used to keep livestock, remain but are not a part of the plantation enterprise. Deriving in part from the couple's Presbyterian background, they maintain both a scientific and a spiritual sense of connection with and obligation to the world and its life forms without claiming a special privilege for humans among other species. There are comparable environmentally maintained projects in neighboring localities, and there is a wildlife conservation area that has been created at the edge of Inch Island, with a walkway right round it enabling views of birds, including numbers of swans and a barrier against the incursion of high waves into the conservation area.

The planting of trees has become a globally popular way of showing concern for the environment, and consciousness about trees has reached communities in Papua New Guinea. In the country's capital city of Port Moresby, the city's mayor Powes Parkop launched in 2019 a campaign to induce environmental awareness among schoolchildren, including clearing up rubbish and tree planting. A government workshop on climate change was held in Mount Hagen in the Highlands region in May 2019, at which an entrepreneur from the neighboring Enga Province reported that for some years he had been planting tree seedlings and distributing or selling these to farming people. He had never received any government funds to assist him in developing this environmentally friendly project, and he asked if government help might be forthcoming.

8 The ends of sustainability

Sustainability means in practice many different things, to different people, according to their values and what is at stake for them. From an ecosystem viewpoint the term should refer to the total survival of all organisms within a given biosphere. In practice discussions usually focus on selected parts of a biosphere, such as agriculture or forest maintenance, or the deleterious effects of industrial activities of mining or manufacture. Through the image of climate change and its hazards for human populations, concerns become globalized to cover the whole planet, and sustainability issues become integrated through all levels of scale. In turn, it is this image of the whole that gives rise to the mobilization of people on an international scale, especially younger people, who aim to save the planet and ensure an econiche for themselves into the future. Complicated issues set in about time and about jobs. It is industrial civilization that has created this situation, along with the growing pressures of food production and the overproduction of people themselves. Thomas Hylland Eriksen has pointed to these kinds of issues in his book *Overheating* (Eriksen 2016). Development has become massive and leads to environmental imbalances that cannot be absorbed by the ecosystem as a whole, hence pollution, toxic effects on species, and a loss of fertility in soil or water. An engine that overheats breaks down or blows up, so the message of Eriksen's title is abundantly clear. In addition, he points to another factor that contributes to ongoing conflicts of interests, which he calls "Clashing Scales". By this he means that what contributes positively to the sustainability of one level of activity may depend on destroying or compromising the sustainability of activity at a different level. We can easily recognize innumerable examples of this negative process from contexts of economic development. Differential power determines the shape of these processes. People may be relocated to make way for an expansion of mining when underground minerals extend into people's dwelling spaces. The removal of a resource such as sand to be used for building materials can disrupt water supplies for people dependent on these. The provision of jobs for one category of people may take away a source of livelihood for others. Given all this, issues of environmental and social justice loom large in any context of arguments about sustainability. This is certainly not a new or unprecedented circumstance, and in fact is intrinsic to the whole history of industrial enterprises and before that to the history of pre-industrial empires. What adds urgency to it today is the global threat of climate change, but ecological reasons for the collapse of complex societies have long entered into the work of historians and comparative scientists.

In these conditions, technological solutions are often brought to the fore. For farming new methods of producing food supplies have been developed, such as hydroponic growing of vegetable supplies for urban consumers, or the production of meat by artificial means, obviating the need to raise stock. We have already discussed the drive for "clean" renewable energy focused on wind, waves, and sunshine, and the pros and cons involved. For automobiles, the development of electric cars or hybrids or cars using fuel cells has been targeted by governments as desirable, similarly for electric-powered planes. Governments set dates for achieving carbon-neutral economies or reducing air pollution. These are all laudable and useful moves, but they still are hampered by the phenomenon of clashing scales identified by Eriksen (2016). Overall population levels are a complicated driving factor. People can be replaced by robots, but robots also require maintenance and are costly to produce and develop.

Ecosystems need mechanisms whereby they can self-monitor and self-modify to keep variables within a certain range, so those in charge of societies today need to develop that capacity of governance, with long-term equilibrium and sustainability as the guiding aim or goal rather than the traditional monetary aim of maximizing profits at the expense of other factors.

A particular contemporary problem highlights the urgency of the themes we have been exploring here. This is the incidence of disasters of an environmental kind. We have worked to develop the studies of these as a new branch of Anthropology and have instituted a book series with Palgrave Macmillan as publishers. Here we sum up some points that underly our aims in starting the series. First, Anthropological studies achieved a high level of competence in understanding and explaining order in societies and the cultural ideas that underpin order. At the same time, it began to be realized that we need to understand processes of rapid change and disorder and how people survive these, as well as studying the conflicts that often emerge in such contexts of change and how peace is reinstated after conflicts. Two massive world wars in the twentieth century and the continuing resurgences of regional wars should be enough to persuade social scientists not to ignore these kinds of phenomena. Wars and environmental disasters produce comparable forms of anomie in terms of material destruction, and climate change scientists have suggested that such disasters may be on the increase, making the study of them imperative. The two components of disaster studies have emerged out of this concern: (1) How can we mitigate the potential effects of adverse weather effects by preparing for them or by guarding against them? and (2) Once a disaster has taken place, how do people adapt to their new situation? These two issues encompass a multitude of problems. In our own work, we distinguish between two phases, one of *coping* with immediate effects of disasters, often at a time of maximum disorder, and *hoping*, the long-term reconstruction of life patterns after the trauma of abrupt rupture precipitated by the event. In this regard, we further draw attention to a vital feature of resilience, the emergence of creative and innovative ways of dealing with the aftermaths of disaster by inventing new crafts, new ways of creating income, and new cultural patterns of leadership and relationality. Hope is made real, even material, in these contexts. We have observed the process often in Taiwan, among indigenous Paiwan-speaking groups that suffered greatly from the destruction caused by Typhoon Morakot in 2009. In one instance a special role was taken up by a female chief of high rank, displaced like many other people from her mountain home by masses of flood water that flushed garden land and trees downhill and onto the coast. Her group's territory extended onto the coastal strip and she had set up a café and craft shop there on the roadside where piles of tree trunks and driftwood had landed up on the shore. The national government of Taiwan had declared that all things that came down with the flood, including timber and gravel, was the property of the state and could not be appropriated by individuals or business groups. This doctrine ran strongly counter to indigenous ideas that forest areas are an extension of their own domains, but it had been established as a state-based rule. However, the Paiwan were not outdone by this rule. The female Paiwan chief said that in general this rule held, but that in this case the logs had landed on her immediate territory, and so were available for people to use. She was allowed to keep the wood and artisans turned these into furniture, while women of her group also worked to devise clothing and traditional-style jewelry, and driftwood furniture was turned into chairs for the coffee shop that she set up to serve tourists.

Another feature of disasters is that they cause a mixing of people and identities as different persons are thrown together in temporary housing or migrate to find new employment outside of their home areas. Conflicts can result, but creative interactions can also emerge. We observed a set of such interactions in the southern city of Taitung in Taiwan, a festive event that brought together people of numbers of indigenous minority Austronesian groups who had all been affected by Morakot. In different stalls they put on rituals reflecting both separate and interconnected aspects of their identities. In addition, shamans from Han Daoist temples performed some of their own rituals. The costumes worn by people also mixed items from more than one ethnic group, with different colors of garments. The whole display advertised a new sense of connections between groups that had collectively suffered from an environmental disaster. The event was experimental, corresponding to a sense of liminality the disaster had caused and at least partly overcoming ethnic divisions. It was a demonstration of the potentiality of ritual to heal and bridge fractures in the social body, thus contributing to the regeneration and sustainability of society.

Our comments here are very much in line with a general theoretical orientation that we have adopted within our anthropological studies that foregrounds the ritualization of responses to crises. This approach is among a number of ways of analyzing such crises and attempts to achieve or restore sustainability of practices. A recent edited collection of studies contains contributions by many prominent scholars and thinkers in social science (Brightman and Lewis 2017). In their Introduction to the volume the editors lay down their view that a radical new set of policies needs to be set in place so as to achieve a livable world for humans and other species in the future. They criticize the concept of "resilience" that is sometimes deployed, saying that it puts pressure on individuals rather than concentrating on needed structural reforms. The leading concept for them is "diversity", meaning that sustainability depends on fostering the diversity of life forms. They are also in favor of local solutions to local problems. An impressive array of contributors follows this challenging set of statements. Bruno Latour is first off, arguing that the term "anthropocene" means that everything that we do in anthropology must change along with this new epoch that humans have created and that physical and cultural anthropologists need to work together to solve the problems for our global survival. In a related vein, Anna Lowenhaupt Tsing argues that environmental problems now threaten the survival and well-being of many species as well as humans and that measures are needed to ensure the resurgence of the multispecies landscapes of life as we know these. Henrietta Moore argues that we should move beyond concerns for indigenous ways of life and look to the broader interdependencies of agencies at all levels and scales of complexity: another global approach. Veronica Strang argues similarly that we need to consider the sustainability of many different species in the world and not just humans who use other species as resources. Arturo Escobar suggests that we should foster the survival of a pluriverse of life forms: a version of concern for the indigenous world. Other contributors look at cases where anthropologists are studying the struggles of ecological movements in frontline contexts or marginal environments. Overall these studies show an effective concentration on the big questions of global survival as well as the ethnographic details of examples from fieldwork indicating the possible contributions of indigenous people themselves to discussions about the future. These studies, then, are in general couched at a broad scale, touching at times on themes that resonate with our own concerns in the present volume. We pick up from there two strands of argument: first, that we can learn from small-scale cases lessons that resonate on wider scales, and, second, that one of the important ways in which rituals work in indigenous cultures is that they function as ecological stabilizers. A focus on the importance of ritual in social life can therefore be fruitfully added to the sociological, historical, and activist agendas of the distinguished contributions to this volume.

References

Aitchison, Peter and Andrew Casswell 2012. *The Lowland Clearances, Scotland's Silent Revolution 1760–1830*. Edinburgh: Birlinn.

Bardhan, Pranab and Isha Ray eds. 2008. *The Contested Commons*. Oxford: Blackwell Publishing.

Barrett, Scott 2018. Choices in the Climate Commons. *Science* 362(6420): 1217.

Brightman, Marc and Jerome Lewis 2017. *Introduction: The Anthropology of Sustainability. Beyond Development and Progress*. New York: Palgrave Macmillan.

Bulmer, Ralph 1982. Traditional Conservation Practices in Papua New Guinea. In: Louise Morauta, John Pernetta, and William Heaney eds. *Traditional Conservation in Papua New Guinea, Implications for Today*, Monograph no. 16, pp. 59–78. Port Moresby: The Institute of Applied Social and Economic Research.

Burton, John 1997. Terra Nugax and the Discovery Paradigm: How Ok Tedi Was Shaped by the Way It Was Found and How the Rise of Political Process in the North Fly Took the Company by Surprise. In: G. Banks and C. Ballard eds. *The Ok Tedi Settlement: Issues, Outcomes and Implications*. Canberra: National Centre for Development Studies and Resource Management in Asia-Pacific, pp. 27–55. The Australian National University, Pacific Policy Paper 27.

Cush, Peter and Aine Macken-Walsh 2016. Farming through the Ages: Joint Farming Ventures in Ireland. *Rural Society*, July: 1–13.

Eriksen, Thomas H. 2016. *Overheating: An Anthropology of Accelerated Change*. London: Pluto Press.

Escobar, Arturo 2017. Sustaining the Pluriverse: The Political Ontology of Territorial Struggles in Latin America. In: M. Brightman and J. Lewis eds. *The Anthropology of Sustainability*. New York: Palgrave Macmillan, pp. 237–256.

Evans-Pritchard, Edward E. 1940. *The Nuer*. Oxford: Oxford University Press.

Feinberg, Richard 2010. Marine Resource Conservation and Prospects for Environmental Sustainability in Anuta, Solomon Islands. *Singapore Journal of Tropical Geography* 31(1): 41–45.

Filer, Colin 1997. West Side Story: The State's and Other Stakes in the Ok Tedi Mine. In: Glenn Banks and Chris Ballard eds. *The Ok Tedi Settlement: Issues, Outcomes and Implications*. Canberra: National Centre for Development Studies and Resource Management in Asia-Pacific, pp. 56–93. The Australian National University, Pacific Policy Paper 27.

Gray, John 2010. Less Favoured Areas in the European Union Pretty and [Un] Economic Landscapes in the Scottish Borders. In: Pamela J. Stewart and Andrew Strathern eds. *Landscape, Heritage, and Conservation: Farming Issues in the European Union*. For, European Anthropology Series. Durham, NC: Carolina Academic Press, pp. 45–74.

Hardin, Garrett 1968. The Tragedy of the Commons. *Science* 162(3859): 1243–1248.

Kerridge, Eric 1992. *The Common Fields of England*. Manchester: Manchester University Press.

Kirsch, Stuart 2014. *Mining Capitalism: The Relationship Between Corporations and Their Critics*. Berkeley: University of California.

Latour, Bruno 2017. Anthropology at the Time of the Anthropocene: A Personal View of What Is to Be Studied. In: M. Brightman and J. Lewis eds. *The Anthropology of Sustainability*. New York: Palgrave Macmillan, pp. 36–49.

Moore, Henrietta 2017. What Can Sustainability Do for Anthropology? In: M. Brightman and J. Lewis eds. *The Anthropology of Sustainability*. New York: Palgrave Macmillan, pp. 67–80.

Morauta, Louise, John Pernetta, and William Heaney eds. 1982. *Traditional Conservation in Papua New Guinea: Implications for Today*. Port Moresby: The Institute for Applied Social and Economic Research, Monograph no. 16.

Ostrom, Elinor 1990. *Governing the Commons: The Evolution of Institutions for Collective Action*. Cambridge: Cambridge University Press.

Ryan, Peter 1991. *Black Bonanza: A Landslide of Gold*. Melbourne: Hyland House.

Sinclair, James 1995. *The Money Tree, Coffee in Papua New Guinea*. Bathurst, NSW: Crawford House Publishing.

Stewart, Pamela J. and Andrew Strathern 2002a. *Remaking the World, Myth, Mining and Ritual Change Among the Duna of Papua New Guinea*. Washington, DC: Smithsonian Institution Press.

Stewart, Pamela J. and Andrew Strathern 2002b. Transformations of Monetary Symbols in the Highlands of Papua New Guinea. Special issue of *L'Homme on Money (Questions de Monnaie)* 162(April/June): 137–156.

Stewart, Pamela J. and Andrew Strathern 2004. *Witchcraft, Sorcery, Rumors, and Gossip*. For, New Departures in Anthropology Series. Cambridge: Cambridge University Press.

Stewart, Pamela J. and Andrew Strathern eds. 2009. *Religious and Ritual Change: Cosmologies and Histories*. For, Ritual Studies Book Series. Durham, NC: Carolina Academic Press.

Stewart, Pamela J. and Andrew Strathern 2010. *Landscape, Heritage, and Conservation: Farming Issues in the European Union*. For, European Anthropology Series. Durham, NC: Carolina Academic Press.

Strang, Veronica 2017. The Gaia Complex: Ethical Challenges to an Anthropocentric "Common Future". In: M. Brightman and J. Lewis eds. *The Anthropology of Sustainability*. New York: Palgrave Macmillan, pp. 207–228.

Strathern, Andrew 2007. *The Rope of Moka.* [Re-Issued with Corrections 2007, original 1971.] Cambridge: Cambridge University Press.

Strathern, Andrew and Pamela J. Stewart 1999. Objects, Relationships, and Meanings: Historical Switches in Currencies in Mount Hagen, Papua New Guinea. In: David Akin and Joel Robbins eds. *Money and Modernity: State and Local Currencies in Melanesia.* Assocation for Social Anthropology in Oceania Monograph Series No. 17. Pittsburgh: University of Pittsburgh Press, pp. 164–191.

Strathern, A. and Pamela J. Stewart 2000. *Arrow Talk: Transaction, Transition, and Contradiction in New Guinea Highlands History.* Kent, OH: Kent State University Press.

Strathern, Andrew and Pamela J. Stewart 2004. *Empowering the Past, Confronting the Future: The Duna People of Papua New Guinea.* New York: Palgrave Macmillan.

Strathern, Andrew and Pamela J. Stewart 2007. Preface to the New Edition. Waves of Change. In: *The Rope of Moka.* [Re-Issued with Corrections, original 1971]. Cambridge: Cambridge University Press, 2007, pp. xv–xviii.

Strathern, Andrew and Pamela J. Stewart 2017. What Is Sustainable? In: Jeremy Caradonna ed. *The Routledge Handbook of the History of Sustainability.* London: Routledge Publishing.

Sutherland, Lee-Ann and Rob F. Burton 2011. Good Farmers, Good Neighbours: The Role of Cultural Capital in Social Capital Development in a Scottish Farming Community. *Sociology Ruralis* 51(3): 238–254.

Tsing, Anna Lowenhaupt 2017. A Threat to Holocene Resurgence Is a Threat to Livability. In: M. Brightman and J. Lewis eds. *The Anthropology of Sustainability*, pp. 51–65. New York: Palgrave Macmillan.

West, Paige 2012. *From Modern Production to Imagined Primitive: The Social World of Coffee from Papua New Guinea.* Durham, NC: Duke University Press.

Wood, Andrew and G.S. Humphreys 1982. Traditional Soil Conservation in Papua New Guinea. In: Louise Morauta, John Pernetta, and William Heaney, eds. *Traditional Conservation in Papua New Guinea. Implications for Today.* Port Moresby: Institute of Applied Social and Economic Research, pp. 93–114.

Index

Printed in the United States
by Baker & Taylor Publisher Services